ESSAYS IN INTERNATIONAL FINANCE
No. 215, August 1999

NO SINGLE CURRENCY REGIME IS RIGHT FOR ALL COUNTRIES OR AT ALL TIMES

JEFFREY A. FRANKEL

INTERNATIONAL FINANCE SECTION
DEPARTMENT OF ECONOMICS
PRINCETON UNIVERSITY
PRINCETON, NEW JERSEY

Library of Congress Cataloging-in-Publication Data

Frankel, Jeffrey A.
No single currency regime is right for all countries or at all times / Jeffrey A. Frankel.
p. cm. — (Essays in international finance ; no. 215)
Includes bibliographical references.
ISBN 0-88165-122-2
1. Monetary unions. 2. Monetary policy. 3. Currency question. I. Series.
HG136.P7 no. 215
[HG3894]
332.4′6—dc21 99-052719
CIP

Printed in the United States of America by Princeton University Printing Services at Princeton, New Jersey

International Standard Serial Number: 0071-142X
International Standard Book Number: 0-88165-122-2
Library of Congress Catalog Card Number: 99-052719

CONTENTS

FIGURES

TABLES

NO SINGLE CURRENCY REGIME IS RIGHT FOR ALL COUNTRIES OR AT ALL TIMES

The sentence chosen for the title of this essay should be vacuous. *Of course* the choice between fixed, floating, or other exchange-rate regimes ought to depend on a country's individual circumstances. But I am not just knocking down a straw man with this statement. Many are now talking as if a global move toward fixed exchange rates, on the one hand, or toward greater flexibility, on the other, would solve a lot of the problems that the international financial system has suffered in recent years.

Among the many observations drawn from the East Asian crisis is the lament that if only these countries had not been pegged to the dollar, none of this would have happened. The list of countries that have been knocked off a dollar peg of one sort of another, typically at great cost, is growing: Mexico, Thailand, Russia, Brazil. Some would argue that the world is, and should be, drawing the lesson that increased flexibility is needed to forestall speculative attacks that lead to deep financial crises and economic recessions. Others claim that if only countries would adopt truly fixed exchange rates, everything would be fine. After all, none of the currencies that fell victim to crises had been literally or formally fixed to the dollar. Enthusiasts point to currency boards that have successfully weathered the storm in Hong Kong and Argentina, and some go even further and suggest full official dollarization. They take encouragement from the euro eleven's successful move to a common currency on January 1, 1999, a transition that has gone more smoothly than most American economists forecast as recently as a few years ago.

I want to make a point stronger than the easy one that no single currency regime is a panacea. Rather, my overall theme is that no single currency regime is best for all countries and that, even for a

---

I would like to thank Barry Eichengreen, David Lipton, and Lawrence Summers for comments, as well as seminar participants at Princeton University, the Massachusetts Institute of Technology, Stanford University, the University of Michigan, the Brookings Institution, the Fletcher School of Law and Diplomacy at Tufts University, the Federal Reserve Bank of New York, the International Monetary Fund, and the Council on Foreign Relations. I thank Ronald Alquist for research assistance.

given country, it may be that no single currency regime is best for all time. I shall also consider the claim that countries are increasingly being pushed to choose between the extremes of a free float or a rigid peg, with the intermediate regimes judged to be no longer tenable.

1 Balancing the Advantages of Fixed and Flexible Exchange Rates

But let's start with the easy point. Neither pure floating nor a currency board sweeps away all the problems that come with modern globalized financial markets. Central to the economists' creed is that life always involves tradeoffs. Countries have to trade off the advantages of more exchange-rate stability against the advantages of more flexibility. Ideally, they will pick the degree of flexibility that optimizes with respect to this exchange. Optimization often, although not always, involves an "interior solution."

The Flexibility Continuum of Exchange-Rate Regimes

"Fixed versus floating" is an oversimplified dichotomy. There is, in fact, a continuum of flexibility, along which it is possible to place most exchange-rate arrangements. Nine such regimes are discussed in this essay, starting with the most rigid regime and progressing to increasingly flexible arrangements:

(1) *Currency union.* In a currency union, the currency that circulates domestically is literally the same as that circulating in one or more major neighbors or partners. Examples of currency unions include Panama and some East Caribbean islands, which use the dollar, and the European Economic and Monetary Union (EMU), which uses the euro. Dollarization has recently been proposed in several Latin American countries. The motivation is to get the maximum credibility for an inflation-resistant monetary policy by adopting the strongest exchange-rate commitment. A currency union is the firmest commitment possible to a fixed exchange rate, but even a currency union can be reversed if desired—witness the Czech and Slovak korunas, whose separation was velvety smooth, and the former Soviet Union, whose division was considerably rougher.

(2) *Currency board.* The currency board, a current fad, is sometimes sold as "credibility in a bottle." Examples of currency boards include Argentina, Hong Kong, and some Eastern European countries. A later section of this paper defines and discusses currency boards at greater length.

(3) *A "truly fixed" exchange rate.* Members of the francophone West African and Central African currency unions fix to the French franc, and many countries fix to the dollar.

(4) *Adjustable peg.* "Fixed but adjustable" was the description of exchange-rate pegs under the Bretton Woods regime. Most countries that declare their rates fixed actually undertake periodic realignments or change regimes altogether.[1]

(5) *Crawling peg.* In high-inflation countries, the peg can be regularly reset in a series of minidevaluations as often as weekly. Chile provides a prominent example of this strategy. Under one variant, which retains a bit of the nominal-anchor function of an exchange-rate target, the path is preannounced. The rate of crawl may be set deliberately lower than the forecasted rate of inflation, in an effort by the country to work its way gradually out of the inflation cycle. This was the case for the *tablita* of the southern cone countries in the late 1970s. Under another strategy, which gives up on fighting inflation and opts instead to live with it, the exchange rate is indexed to the price level in an attempt to keep the real exchange rate steady.

(6) *Basket peg.* In a basket peg, the exchange rate is fixed in terms of a weighted basket of foreign currencies, instead of any one major currency, a strategy that makes sense for countries with trade patterns that are highly diversified geographically, as many in Asia are. In theory, there is little reason why this arrangement cannot be as rigid as an exchange rate fixed to one single currency. In practice, most countries that announce a basket peg keep the weights secret and adjust the weights or the level sufficiently often that the formula cannot be precisely inferred. An exception is the handful of countries that peg to the special drawing right (SDR).

(7) *Target zone or band.* With a target zone or band, the authorities pledge to intervene when the exchange rate hits preannounced margins on either side of a central parity. An example is the exchange-rate mechanism (ERM) of the European Monetary System (EMS) from its founding in 1979 until EMU in 1999, under which a number of European countries contained their currencies within a band of plus or minus 2.25 percent (still maintained by Denmark). If the band is

[1] Obstfeld and Rogoff (1995) report that only six major economies with open capital markets, and a number of very small economies, had maintained a fixed exchange rate for five or more years as of 1995. Klein and Marion (1997) report that the mean duration of pegs among Western Hemisphere countries is about ten months.

sufficiently narrow, a target zone approaches a fixed rate (such as the 1 percent width that ruled under the Bretton Woods system and that is still the official definition of a fixed peg). If sufficiently wide, it approaches a float (such as the 15 percent width of the ERM after 1993, which is still maintained by Greece).[2]

(8) *Managed float.* Also known as a "dirty float," a managed float is defined as a readiness to intervene in the foreign-exchange market, without defending any particular parity. Most intervention is intended to lean against the wind—buying the currency when it is rising (or is already high) and selling when it is falling (or is already low). In a stylized version, a managed floater responds to a 1 percent change in demand for his currency by partial accommodation—changing the supply of the currency by K percent and letting the rest of the change in demand show up in the price, the exchange rate. When K is close to 1, the exchange rate is fixed; when it is close to 0, the rate is floating.

(9) *Free float.* With a free float, the central bank does not intervene in the foreign-exchange market but, instead, allows private supply and demand to clear on their own. (Even then, there is the question about the extent to which monetary policy responds to exchange-rate objectives.) The United States comes closest to a pure example of a free float.

The Hypothesis of the Vanishing Intermediate Regime

Nonideologues look at recent history and agree that both free floating and rigid fixity have flaws. Nevertheless, many increasingly hypothesize that intermediate regimes seem no longer to be tenable. The currently fashionable view is that countries are being pushed to choose between the extremes of truly fixed and truly floating exchange-rate regimes.[3] For example, Lawrence Summers (1999) stated that:

[2] Target zones come in two varieties, depending on whether the central parity is fixed in nominal terms (as in the formal model of Krugman, 1991) or is adjusted with inflation and economic fundamentals (as in the proposal of Williamson, 1985).

[3] The original references on the vanishing intermediate regime are Eichengreen (1994, 1998). In the context of the European ERM, the crisis of 1992 and band-widening of 1993 suggested to some that a gradual transition to EMU, in which the width of the target zone was narrowed in steps, might not be the best way to proceed after all (Crockett, 1994). Obstfeld and Rogoff (1995, p. 74) concluded that "a careful examination of the genesis of speculative attacks suggests that even broad-band systems in the current EMS style pose difficulties, and that there is little, if any, comfortable middle ground between floating rates and the adoption by countries of a common currency" (see also Goldstein, 1995, pp. 9–10). The lesson that the best way to cross a chasm is in a single jump was seemingly borne out by the successful leap from wide bands to EMU in 1998–99.

there is no single answer, but in light of recent experience what is perhaps becoming increasingly clear—and will probably be increasingly reflected in the advice that the international community offers—is that in a world of freely flowing capital there is shrinking scope for countries to occupy the middle ground of fixed but adjustable pegs. As we go forward from the events of the past eighteen months, I expect that countries will be increasingly wary about committing themselves to fixed exchange rates, whatever the temptations these may offer in the short run, unless they are also prepared to dedicate policy wholeheartedly to their support and establish extraordinary domestic safeguards to keep them in place.

Although there are understandable reasons for this view, the generalization is in danger of being overdone. Of 185 economies, the International Monetary Fund (IMF) classifies 47 as independently floating and 45 as following rigid pegs (currency boards or monetary unions, including the franc zone in Africa). That leaves 93 economies following intermediate regimes. Most of those classified as fixed have, in fact, had realignments within the last ten years. Even the francophone countries of Africa finally devalued against the French franc in 1994. Similarly, most of those listed as floating in fact intervene frequently in the foreign-exchange market. Only the United States floats so purely that intervention is relatively rare. Most countries still choose something between rigid fixity and free float, and perhaps for good reason.[4] Again, close to the center of the economists' creed is the belief that interior solutions are more likely—for the interesting questions—than corner solutions.

What, then is the origin of the hypothesis of the disappearing intermediate regime (the "missing middle")? At first glance, it appears to be a corollary to the principle of the impossible trinity. That principle says that a country must give up one of three goals—exchange-rate stability, monetary independence, or financial-market integration; it cannot have all three simultaneously. If one adds the observation that financial markets are steadily becoming more and more integrated internationally, the choice is narrowed to giving up on exchange-rate stability or giving up on monetary independence. But this is not the same thing as saying one cannot give up on *both*, that one cannot have half-stability and half-independence. There is nothing in existing theory, for example, that prevents a country from pursuing a managed float under which half of

[4] The intermediate regimes in the IMF classification scheme broke down as follows on January 1, 1999: 25 pegged to a single currency, 13 pegged to a composite, 6 crawling pegs, 12 horizontal bands, 10 crawling bands, and 26 managed floats (*International Financial Statistics*, April 1999).

every fluctuation in the demand for its currency is accommodated by intervention and half is reflected in the exchange rate.

Figure 1 is a simple schematic illustration of the impossible trinity. Each of the three sides has an attraction—the respective allure of monetary independence, exchange-rate stability, and full financial integration. One can attain any pair of attributes: the first two at the apex marked "capital controls," the second two at the vertex marked "monetary union," or the first and third at the vertex marked "pure float." But one cannot be on all three sides simultaneously. The general trend of financial integration has pushed most countries toward the lower part of the figure. If one is at the bottom leg of the triangle, the choice is limited to a simple decision regarding the degree of exchange-rate flexibility. But even under perfect capital mobility, there is nothing to prevent a country from choosing an intermediate solution between floating and monetary union.

Recent history explains why some would flee the soft middle ground of regimes 4 through 7 listed above and seek the bedrock of the extremes 1, 2, 8, or 9. Monetary union and pure floating are the two regimes that cannot by construction be subjected to speculative attack. Most of the intermediate regimes have been tried and have failed, often spectacularly so. Contrary to claims that Mexico, Thailand, Indonesia, Korea, Russia or Brazil were formally pegged to the dollar when they suffered recent crises, these countries were using a variety of bands, baskets, and crawling pegs. Perhaps when international investors are lacking in confidence and risk-tolerance—conditions that have characterized the response to emerging markets since 1997—governments can reclaim confidence only by proclaiming policies that are so simple and so transparent that investors can verify instantly that the government is in fact doing what it claims it is doing. If a central bank, for example, announces a band around a crawling basket peg,[5] it takes a surprisingly large number of daily observations for a market participant to solve the statistical problem, either explicitly or implicitly, of estimating the parameters (the weights in the basket, the rate of the crawl, and the width of the band) and thus testing the hypothesis that the central bank is abiding by its announced regime. This is particularly true if the central bank does not announce the weights in the basket (as is usually the case) or other parameters. By contrast, market participants can instantly verify the announcement of a simple dollar peg.

[5] Israel and Chile, for example, have, during the 1990s, had crawling bands around basket pegs (Williamson, 1996).

FIGURE 1

THE IMPOSSIBLE TRINITY

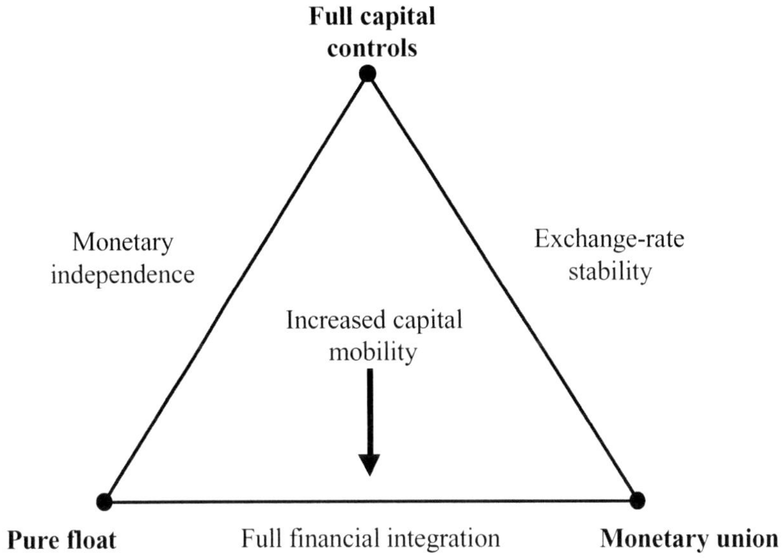

An alternative interpretation is that the search for a single regime that will eliminate currency speculation as an issue is a search that cannot be successful (short of capital restrictions). Large swings and speculative bubbles will occasionally intrude on the nirvana of pure floating.[6] Even the central bankers' oblivion of monetary union will not offer an end to earthly sorrows, because political upheavals will occasionally intrude from time to time. The rejection of the middle ground is explained simply as a rejection of where most countries have been, with no reasonable expectation that the dreamed-of sanctuaries, monetary union or free floating, will be any better. The grass will always be greener on the other side of the parity. Many countries will be fated to switch back and forth among various regimes, in an unending Markov process. If this interpretation is right, the only advice one can give most central

[6] What would have happened if the emerging-market currencies of East Asia had floated freely throughout the 1990s? They would probably have appreciated strongly through 1996, producing even larger current-account deficits than actually occurred. The crisis, when it came, would have taken a different form—a burst bubble—but might arguably have been even worse than it was if larger international debts had been run up in the meantime.

bankers in vulnerable countries is to stay on their toes.[7] A blanket recommendation to avoid the middle regimes would not be appropriate.

Reminder of the Advantages of Fixed Compared with Floating Regimes

This is not the place to enter into an extended discussion of the relative advantages of fixed and floating exchange rates. The main points can be stated succinctly. The two big advantages of a fixed exchange rate, for any country, are (1) that it reduces transactions costs and exchange-rate risk, which can discourage trade and investment, and (2) that it provides a credible nominal anchor for monetary policy. The big advantage of a floating exchange rate is that it enables a country to pursue an independent monetary policy.[8]

Twenty or thirty years ago, the argument most often made against floating currencies was that higher exchange-rate variability would create uncertainty; this risk would in turn discourage international trade and investment. Fixing the exchange rate in terms of a large neighbor would eliminate exchange-rate risk and thus encourage international trade and investment. Going one step further and actually adopting the neighbor's currency as one's own would eliminate transactions costs as well and would thereby promote trade and investment still more.

Most academic economists tend to downplay this argument today. One reason is that exchange-rate risk can be hedged through the use of the forward exchange market and other instruments. (Although there are costs to hedging, in terms of both bid-ask spread and a possible exchange-risk premium, these are generally thought to be small.) Another reason is that there have been quite a few empirical studies of the effect of exchange-rate volatility on trade, as well as some on investment. Most of these studies find small adverse effects, if they find any at all.[9]

[7] The exceptions where the economies are suited to corner solutions include Estonia, Hong Kong, and Panama, on the one hand, and Japan, the United States, and euroland as a whole, on the other.

[8] To be sure, other factors enter as well. Another advantage of fixed exchange rates, for example, is that they prevent competitive depreciation or competitive appreciation. Two other advantages of an independent currency are that the government retains seigniorage, and floating allows smooth adjustment to real shocks even in the presence of price frictions. Most of the important factors, however, can be lumped into the major arguments presented in the text.

[9] Surveys of the literature are included in Edison and Melvin (1990) and Goldstein (1995, pp. 53–63). A recent cross-sectional approach that finds statistically significant effects of bilateral exchange-rate variability on bilateral trade in the 1960s and 1970s can

This argument nevertheless still carries some weight. It looms large in the minds of European policymakers and business people. Promoting trade and investment in Europe was certainly a prime motivation for EMU. Furthermore, there has been no satisfactory testing of the proposition that trade and investment are substantially boosted by full monetary union: when political units share a common currency, even the possibility of a future change in the exchange rate is eliminated, along with all transactions costs. Some recent tests of economic geography suggest that Canadian provinces are far more closely linked to each other then they are to nearby states of the United States, whether the links are measured by prices or by quantities of trade. High on the list of reasons why integration seems to be so much higher among provinces within a federation such as Canada than between countries is the fact that the provinces share a common currency.[10]

Of the advantages of fixed exchange rates, academic economists tend to focus most on the nominal anchor for monetary policy. The argument is that there can be an inflationary bias when monetary policy is set with full discretion. A central bank that wants to fight inflation can commit more credibly by fixing the exchange rate, or even by giving up its currency altogether. Workers, firm managers, and others who set wages and prices then perceive that inflation will be low in the future, because the currency peg will prevent the central bank from expanding the money supply even if it wants to (without soon jeopardizing the viability of the exchange-rate peg). When workers and firm managers have low expectations of inflation, they set their wages and prices accordingly. The result is that the country is able to attain a lower level of inflation for any given level of output. This explains why countries such as Italy, Portugal, and Spain, which had high inflation rates in the 1970s, were eager to tie their currencies to those of Germany and the rest of the EMS countries. They hoped to import the inflation-fighting credibility of the Bundesbank. The nominal-anchor argument presupposes, of course, a peg to a hard currency, one that exhibits strong monetary discipline. After the breakup of the Soviet Union, most of the fifteen newly independent states wisely discerned that the Russian ruble did not offer a good nominal anchor. The strength of the argu-

be found in the studies by Frankel and Wei (1995) and Frankel (1997, pp. 137–139). The negative effect disappears, however, after 1980.

[10] See McCallum (1995) for a quantity-based measure of trade integration and Engel and Rogers (1996, 1998) for a price-based measure. The most direct test yet of the effect of a common currency on bilateral trade is Rose (1999).

ment for basing monetary policy on an exchange-rate target will also depend on the availability of alternative nominal anchors such as money supply, nominal income, and price level.

The advantages of a flexible exchange rate can all be grouped under one main property: it allows the country to pursue an independent monetary policy. The argument in favor of monetary independence, instead of constraining monetary policy by the fixed exchange rate, is the classical argument for discretion instead of rules. When the economy is hit by a disturbance, such as a shift in worldwide demand away from the goods it produces, the government would like to be able to respond, so that the country does not go into recession. Under fixed exchange rates, monetary policy is always diverted, at least to some extent, to dealing with the balance of payments. Under the combination of fixed exchange rates and complete integration of financial markets, a condition that characterizes EMU, monetary policy becomes completely powerless. Under these conditions, the domestic interest rate is tied to the foreign interest rate. An expansion in the money supply has no effect, because the new money flows out of the country, by way of a balance-of-payments deficit, just as quickly as it is created. In the face of an adverse disturbance, the country must simply live with the effects. After the fall in demand, for example, the recession may last until wages and prices are bid down, or until some other automatic mechanism of adjustment takes hold. By freeing up the currency, however, the country can respond to a recession by means of monetary expansion and depreciation of the currency. This stimulates demand for domestic products and returns the economy to desired levels of employment and output more rapidly than would occur under the automatic mechanisms of adjustment on which a fixed-rate country must rely.

The argument for stabilizing the exchange rate is sometimes buttressed by reference to an increasingly evident disadvantage of free floating: a tendency toward volatility that does not always derive from macroeconomic fundamentals and that includes occasional speculative bubbles (possibly rational, possibly not) and crashes. The argument for flexibility, however, is sometimes correspondingly buttressed by reference to an increasingly evident disadvantage of pegging: a tendency for borrowers' effectively unhedged exposure in foreign currency (possibly rational, possibly not) to end badly in speculative attacks.[11] Overvaluation and excessive volatility are possible in either regime.

[11] Many who have recently argued for floating on these grounds verge on implying that it would be beneficial to introduce gratuitous volatility into the exchange rate, to discourage unhedged borrowing in foreign currencies.

Which factors are likely to dominate, the advantages of fixed exchange rates or the advantages of floating? There is no one right answer for all countries. The response must depend, in large part, on the characteristics of the country in question. If the country is subject to many external disturbances, for example, such as fluctuations in foreigners' eagerness to buy domestic goods and domestic assets (perhaps arising from business-cycle fluctuations among the country's neighbors), it is more likely to want to float its currency. In this way, it can insulate itself from foreign disturbances to some degree. If the country is subject to many internal disturbances, however, it is more likely to want to peg its currency.

2 No Single Currency Regime is Right for All Countries: The Optimum Currency Area

Many of the characteristics that are most important to the fixed-versus-floating question are closely related to the size and openness of the country. This observation brings us to the theory of the optimum currency area (OCA); see Tavlas, 1993, for a recent survey, as well as Bayoumi and Eichengreen, 1994.

Definition of an Optimum Currency Area

Countries that are highly integrated with each other, with respect to trade and other economic relationships, are most likely to constitute an optimum currency area. An optimum currency area is a region for which it is optimal to have a single currency and a single monetary policy. This definition, though in common use, may be too broad to be of optimum use. It can be enhanced by asserting that smaller units tend to be more open and integrated with their neighbors than are larger units.[12] An optimum currency area can thus be defined as a region that is neither so small and open that it would be better off pegging its currency to a neighbor, nor so large that it would be better off splitting into subregions with different currencies. The principle of the interior solution crops up again. Even to the extent that corner solutions are appropriate for given countries, the optimal geographic coverage for a common currency is likely to be intermediate in size: larger than a city and smaller than the entire planet.

[12] Gravity estimates suggest that for every 1 percent increase in the size of a country's economy (holding constant income per capita), its ratio of trade to gross domestic product (GDP) falls by about 0.3 percent (Frankel, 1997, p. 64).

The Integration Parameters of the OCA Criterion

Why does the OCA criterion depend on openness? The advantages of fixed exchange rates increase with the degree of economic integration, whereas the advantages of flexible exchange rates diminish. Recall the two big advantages mentioned above of a fixed exchange rate: (1) the reduction of transactions costs and exchange-rate risk, which can discourage trade and investment, and (2) the provision of a credible nominal anchor for monetary policy. Where traded goods constitute a large proportion of the economy, exchange-rate uncertainty is a more serious issue for the country in the aggregate.[13] Such an economy may be too small and too open to support an independently floating currency. At the same time, because fixing the exchange rate in such an economy goes further toward fixing the entire price level, an exchange-rate peg is more likely to be credible and thus more likely to succeed in reducing inflationary expectations (Romer, 1993).

The chief advantage of a floating exchange rate, moreover, the ability to pursue an independent monetary policy, is in many ways weaker for a country that is highly integrated with its neighbors. This is because there are ways that such a country or region can cope with an adverse shock even in the absence of discretionary changes in macroeconomic policy. Consider first, as the criterion for openness, the marginal propensity to import. Variability in output and the price level under a fixed exchange rate is relatively low when the marginal propensity to import is high; openness acts as an automatic stabilizer.

Consider next, as the criterion for openness, the ease of labor movement between the country in question and its neighbors. If the economy is highly integrated with its neighbors by this criterion, workers may be able to respond to a local recession by moving across the border to get jobs. There is therefore less need for a local monetary expansion or devaluation.[14]

Of course, the neighbor may be in recession at the same time. To the extent that shocks to the two economies are correlated, however, monetary independence is not needed: the two can share a monetary expansion in tandem. There is less need for a flexible exchange rate between them to accommodate differences.

Consider, finally, a rather special kind of integration: the existence of a federal fiscal system to transfer funds to regions that suffer adverse

[13] This is the rationale for the openness criterion originally suggested by McKinnon (1963).

[14] Labor mobility was the criterion identified by Mundell (1961), who originally introduced the concept of the optimum currency area.

shocks. The existence of such a system, like the existence of high labor mobility or high correlation of shocks, makes monetary independence less necessary.

Stretching the definition of integration even further, another kind of integration, more political in nature, can help reduce the need for monetary independence. To the extent that domestic residents have economic priorities that are similar to those of their neighbors—especially about fighting inflation rather than fighting unemployment—there will be less need for a differentiated response to common shocks (Corden, 1972; Alesina and Grilli, 1992). To the extent that individuals think of themselves as citizens of Europe more than as citizens of their own country, they may be willing on political grounds to forego discretionary monetary responses even to disturbances that are so large that a national policy response would be to their economic advantage. Conversely, to the extent that they prize their national sovereignty, they will not want to give up their national currency even if it is economically advantageous.

Section 5 of this essay focuses on two OCA criteria in particular, the extent of trade among members of a given group and the correlation of their incomes. The two axes in Figure 2 represent these two parameters. The OCA line is downward-sloping: the advantages of adopting a common currency depend positively on trade integration, and the disadvantages of abandoning monetary independence (which is the same thing) depend negatively on income correlation.[15] Points high up and to the right represent groups that should adopt a common currency among themselves; points down and to the left represent groups that should float.

3 Corner Solutions Are Right for Some Countries

A popular hypothesis is that the world monetary system will feature fewer currencies in the coming decade than it does now. Small open countries (and perhaps not only these) will abandon their independent currencies in favor of the firmest institutional constraints possible, either a currency board or an outright monetary union with one of the major-currency countries. One version of the hypothesis overlaps with the familiar claim that the world is breaking up into three blocs, one pegged to the dollar, one to the euro, and one to the yen.[16]

[15] Effective capital controls are assumed not to be an option. Thus, fixing the exchange rate implies abandoning the ability to set the interest rate independently.

[16] The dollar and euro are looking somewhat more credible as bloc anchors than they have in the past. The yen looks much less so (Frankel and Wei, 1995).

FIGURE 2

Two Key Parameters in the OCA Criterion

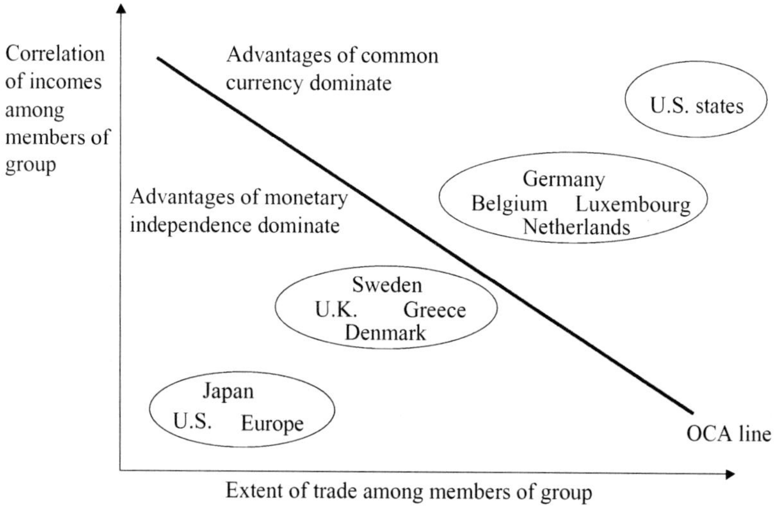

Currency Boards

A currency board is a monetary institution that issues currency only that is fully backed by foreign assets. Its principal attributes include:

- an exchange rate fixed not just by policy, but by law;
- a reserve requirement stipulating that each dollar's worth of domestic currency is backed by a dollar's worth of foreign reserves;
- a self-correcting balance-of-payments mechanism, in which a payments deficit automatically contracts the money supply, resulting in a contraction of spending.

The first currency board was established by the British in Mauritius in 1849, and the use of currency boards eventually spread to seventy British colonies. The purpose of these boards was to provide the colonies with a stable currency without the associated difficulty of issuing sterling notes and coins that were costly to replace if lost or destroyed. The colonies also benefited from this strategy in that they could earn interest on the foreign-currency assets being held in reserve. The use of currency boards peaked in the 1940s and declined thereafter. In the 1960s, many newly independent African countries replaced their currency boards with central banks, and most other countries followed suit in the 1970s.

The recent introduction of arrangements similar to currency boards in Hong Kong (1983), Argentina (1991), Estonia (1992), Lithuania (1994), Bulgaria (1997), and Bosnia (1998) constitutes a resurgence in their use. Proponents should get credit for taking an intellectual idea seriously enough to put it into practice, at a time when most economists either were skeptical of currency boards or did not even know what they were. A currency board can help to create a credible policy environment by removing from the monetary authorities the option of printing money to finance government deficits. Argentina, for example, which was prompted to adopt a currency board (which it calls the "convertibility plan") in response to a dramatic hyperinflation in the 1980s and the absence of a reliable monetary authority, has benefited from such credibility. Since 1991, Argentina has become a model of price stability and has achieved laudable growth rates, aside from such setbacks as the sharp recession in 1995 induced by the "tequila crisis," the Mexican peso crisis, from which Argentina rebounded quickly and strongly. By most accounts, the currency board has worked for Argentina.

Yet, Argentina does not fit well the traditional OCA criteria. It is not particularly small or open, and it is not subject to high labor mobility or to close correlation with the U.S. economy. Although the traditional OCA criteria are still relevant, recent developments have suggested that a new set of criteria is also pertinent, particularly to the decision to adopt an institutional commitment to a fixed rate. The new criteria relate to credibility and the need to satisfy international financial markets. They are:[17]

- a strong, even desperate, need to import monetary stability, owing to either a history of hyperinflation, an absence of credible public institutions, or an unusually large exposure to nervous international investors;
- a desire for further close integration with a particular neighbor or trading partner; this has the added advantage of enhancing the political credibility of the commitment;
- an economy in which the foreign currency is already widely used;[18]
- access to an adequate level of reserves;

[17] Similar lists are offered by Williamson (1995) and Larraín and Velasco (1999).

[18] In a country that is already partly dollarized, devaluation is of little use. If many wages and prices are already tied to the dollar, they will simply rise by the same amount as the exchange rate. If liabilities are already denominated in dollars—and, in the case of international liabilities of developing countries, foreign creditors generally insist on this—devaluation may bankrupt domestic borrowers. Such "initial conditions" are discussed as criteria for dollarization by Calvo (1999) and Hausmann et al. (1999).

- the rule of law; and
- a strong, well-supervised, and regulated financial system.

Currency-board supporters have recently pushed for their wider use—specifically, in Indonesia, Russia, and Ukraine. Proclaiming a currency board, however, does not automatically guarantee the credibility of the fixed-rate peg. Little credibility is gained by inserting an exchange-rate peg into the laws of a country where laws are not heeded or are changed at will. A currency board is also unlikely to be successful without the solid fundamentals of adequate reserves, fiscal discipline, and a strong and well-supervised financial system (see Williamson, 1995, for a balanced evaluation).

The Alternative of Dollarization

Currency boards, which not long ago appeared to be a radical straitjacket, are now in some quarters deemed an insufficiently firm commitment. In January 1999, at the request of Argentina's president, the Argentine central bank submitted a report spelling out possible ways to complete the dollarization of that country, that is, to replace the peso fully with the dollar as the legal currency. This plan may never come to fruition. The timing of the initiative—immediately after the downfall of the real in neighboring Brazil and in advance of a presidential election in Argentina—suggests the influence of possible short-term objectives, such as the need to impress contagion-prone speculators and stability-craving voters. Many Latin Americans are nevertheless suddenly taking the dollarization alternative seriously—in Central America, for example. The fact that anyone would consider that talk of official dollarization might earn the Argentine president political popularity, rather than the reverse, is itself a sign of how much the world has changed.[19]

The reasons why most countries would not want to adopt as their own the currency of the United States or of any other foreign power are clear. It would be a total surrender of monetary independence. In addition, it would mean the surrender of an emblem of national political sovereignty, a demonstrably important symbol to most people. It is striking that, although in theory, the boundaries of political units and optimal currency areas need not coincide, in practice, they almost always do. In Israel in 1983, adverse popular reaction to the idea of dollarization was severe, and the finance minister who had proposed it resigned.

[19] Another respect in which the popularity of dollarization might to some extent be specific to the late 1990s is the tremendous reputation enjoyed by U.S. monetary policy during the Greenspan chairmanship and Clinton economic boom.

Yet, consider a country in which a foreign currency already plays a large role in the economy and which has already demonstrated sufficient political support for monetary discipline to have installed a currency board. Is there anything more for this country to lose by going the rest of the way and giving up its national currency completely, beyond the symbolic loss of sovereignty?

The conventional interpretation would be that such a country still retains a degree of monetary independence that, although small, is not zero, and that it would be giving up this independence if it were to dollarize fully. Argentina, for example, can always change its convertibility law if it chooses to or, short of that, switch its peg from the dollar to the euro, if U.S. monetary policy disappoints.[20]

The unfortunate truth is that most developing countries have been unable to make good use of whatever monetary independence they possess. Perhaps the additional loss of discretionary monetary policy for Argentina would be not just small, but zero. Perhaps an emerging-market country under a fixed exchange rate or currency board is in a worse position than it would be under dollarization by having to accept an interest rate that may not be appropriate to its current domestic cyclical conditions. Under the current regime, when the U.S. Federal Reserve Board raises interest rates in the United States, emerging-market interest rates often rise more than one for one. The differential between Argentine and U.S. interest rates declined after the April 1991 convertibility plan and has been relatively small most of the time since 1993. Nevertheless, it is still nonnegligible. The differential is sensitive to external disturbances such as contagion from crises in other emerging markets, as well as changes in U.S. interest rates. Renewed sharp spikes following the tequila crisis of December 1994 and Russian crisis of August 1998 illustrated the point dramatically. When the U.S. interest rate increases, the Argentine interest rate increases more than one for one. A regression produces the result that when the U.S. federal funds rate rises 1 basis point, the Argentine dollar interest rate rises, on average, an estimated 2.73 basis points (see Table 1); the result is statistically significant.[21]

[20] Furthermore, Argentina actually has a "quasi" currency board, which can, in effect, sterilize a certain portion of reserve outflows by allowing banks to acquire domestic dollar-denominated bonds as reserves.

[21] The sample period runs from November 1994, when the dollar-denominated instrument was first available, to December 1998. If one responds to borderline serial correlation by taking first differences, the estimated coefficient drops to 0.88. For Hong Kong, the estimated coefficient is just above 1 (although insignificantly so), regardless of

The interest-rate differential consists primarily of a country premium, supplemented by a small currency premium. The country premium is compensation for the perceived risk of default, measured as the Argentine dollar interest rate minus the U.S. Treasury bill rate. The currency premium is compensation for the perceived risk of a change in exchange-rate policy, measured as the Argentine peso interest rate minus the dollar-denominated Argentine interest rate. We used to think of countries' currency premiums and country premiums as independent factors. We have learned, however, that when fears of devaluation linger, they affect not only the currency premium, but the country premium as well, because investors know that domestic banks and firms may not be able to service their dollar debts in the event of a devaluation.

The currency premium would, by definition, vanish if Argentina were to dollarize. It is true that the country premium would not vanish, but it might diminish or become less sensitive to foreign disturbances when the possibility of devaluation disappears. The interesting hypothesis in Table 1 is that under dollarization, the regression coefficient on foreign interest rates would be smaller. For purposes of comparison, consider Panama. The hypothesis is borne out. When the U.S. federal funds rate rises 1 basis point, the Panamanian interest rate rises, on average, only an estimated 0.43 basis points (in terms of first differences, the coefficient is 0.40). The suggested implication is that, somewhat paradoxically, Argentina might be less at the mercy of the Federal Reserve if it were to go on the dollar standard. But a drawback would be that increases in Argentine interest rates would bear U.S. fingerprints more visibly from a political standpoint; the statistical fit is tighter for the dollarized country than for the currency-board country.

The same pattern holds when the tests are extended to two Latin American countries with less firm ties to the dollar. When short-term interest rates in Brazil and Mexico are regressed against the U.S. federal funds rate, the estimated coefficients are substantially higher, even, than they were for Argentina.[22] But the standard errors are also

---

taking first differences or not. For each currency considered, one cannot reject the hypothesis of a unit root. A need for first differences is conventionally indicated by this result, which, however, could be due to low power.

[22] Similar results regarding the behavior of interest rates in fixed as opposed to flexible regimes are found by Hausmann et al. (1999). The finding that interest rates in emerging markets react more than one for one to U.S. short-term interest rates is not new. More results and references are given in Frankel and Okongwu (1996). Tests of monetary stability under various exchange-rate regimes are found in Ghosh et al. (1997).

TABLE 1

REGRESSIONS OF LOCAL INTEREST RATES AGAINST THE U.S. FEDERAL FUNDS RATE

Country	Period (Monthly or Quarterly)	Specification	Constant	Coefficient	Durbin-Watson	R^2	Mean of Dependent Variable	SER
Argentina	1994:10–1998:12	Money-market rate for U.S. dollars: level	–8.11 (4.38)	2.73[a] (0.80)	1.48	0.19	6.83	1.66
Argentina	1994:11–1998:12	Money-market rate for U.S. dollars: first difference	—	0.88 (1.90)	2.91	0.00	0.01	2.00
Brazil	1995:1–1998:6	T-bill rate: level	–221.13 (7.36)	45.93[a] (5.43)	1.12	0.64	32.78	8.42
Brazil	1995:2–1998:6	T-bill rate: first difference	—	12.96 (11.15)	2.61	0.03	–0.49	8.08
Hong Kong	1993:12–1998:12	Money-market rate: level	0.27 (1.57)	1.03[a] (0.30)	1.70	0.17	5.63	1.68
Hong Kong	1994:1–1998:12	Money-market rate: first difference	—	1.09 (1.73)	2.97	0.01	0.03	2.19
Mexico	1994:10–1998:12	Money-market rate: level	–112.65 (35.67)	26.65[a] (6.51)	0.43	0.25	33.07	13.50
Mexico	1994:10–1998:12	Money-market rate: first difference	—	15.77[b] (8.17)	1.78	0.07	0.40	8.63
Mexico	1994:10–1998:12	T-bill rate: level	–98.98 (31.81)	23.62[a] (5.81)	0.34	0.25	30.17	12.04
Mexico	1994:10–1998:12	T-bill rate: first difference	—	14.21[c] (6.46)	1.61	0.09	0.39	6.82
Panama	1986:I–1998:II	Deposit rate: level	4.47 (0.29)	0.43[a] (0.05)	0.82	0.64	6.99	0.58
Panama	1986:II–1998:II	Deposit rate: first difference	—	0.40[c] (0.16)	2.93	0.12	0.02	0.52

NOTE: Standard errors are reported in parentheses.

[a] Coefficient is significant at the 1 percent level.

[b] Coefficient is significant at the 10 percent level.

[c] Coefficient is significant at the 5 percent level.

larger. It seems, unusually, as if the looser the relationship, the higher the regression coefficient. This supports the notion that the presence of exchange-rate uncertainty exacerbates swings in the risk premium.

The Argentine Dollarization Proposal: Is It a Good Idea?

The blueprint devised by the Argentine authorities details three possible approaches to dollarization: bilaterally negotiated (through a "treaty of monetary association" with the United States), unilateral, and regional.

There are three things that the Argentines might hope to get out of a negotiated agreement. They are not expected to ask for a fourth, voting rights on the Federal Reserve Open Market Committee, as the eleven euro countries have at the European Central Bank (ECB). Full dollarization is thus a different kind of monetary union than EMU is.

The first thing the Argentines have asked for is a return of their lost seigniorage, worth about $600 million to $750 million, measured as the interest that the central bank now earns by holding $14 billion of foreign-exchange reserves (U.S. Treasury bills) against domestic peso liabilities.[23] The second is access by Argentine banks to the Federal discount window. The third is cooperation regarding bank supervision. The United States is quite unlikely to agree to compensate Argentina for lost seigniorage, or to agree to open-ended access to the discount window, even with the Argentine proposal to use donated seigniorage funds to collateralize borrowing by its banks. Cooperative exchange of information in the area of banking supervision is more likely, especially if U.S. banks continue to play a growing role in the Argentine banking system. The United States is so wary of incurring a contingent liability, however, that it may refuse to enter into even a symbolic treaty designed to give a stamp of approval to the plan, for fear of creating implicit expectations of future bailouts.

Argentina could choose, instead, to dollarize unilaterally. Given its proven historical inability to put monetary policy to good use, dollarization might be advantageous to Argentina, even without help on seigniorage or lender-of-last resort facilities, provided the loss of sovereignty is politically acceptable.

Would Argentine dollarization be beneficial to the United States? To say that the effect would be very small is true but not helpful. The next step would be to ask what the effect would be if other countries were also to dollarize. Because the effects would start to add up, we had

[23] Argentina's seigniorage is already smaller than it would be for many countries, because it has already given up the domestic credit component of seigniorage. Note that here and throughout, "billion" equals one thousand million.

better consider their desirability now. For the United States, economic benefits would include seigniorage, enhanced ease of transactions in Argentina for U.S. businesses and travelers, and the increased trade that stability and prosperity in the area would bring about. There might also be foreign-policy benefits to spreading U.S. influence, although imperialism is distinctly out of fashion. The only obvious drawback for the United States would be the danger of implicit bailout liabilities, which might occur even without the official sanction provided by a treaty. Still, the benefits probably outweigh the costs. This is especially true because the United States already bears some responsibility for leadership when international financial crises strike, and the probability of a crisis in Argentina would presumably be reduced under a dollarization plan. If this evaluation of U.S. costs and benefits is correct, the idea might merit an American blessing, even if that blessing must be unofficial. Corner solutions are *sometimes* right.

The last question is what the costs or benefits would be of a regional move to dollarization. Clearly, the failure of Brazil's link to the dollar in January 1999 threatened Argentina financially, and the change in the real exchange rate disrupted trade relations among the Mercosur partners. The benefits to one country of a firmer dollar link are enhanced if others move in the same direction. But this externality is a very general aspect of the benefits of money: a given currency is always more convenient to use if others use it. There is little reason to forecast a mass regional movement to the dollar at this point in history merely on the grounds that it would gather steam as it goes. Countries with a past history of hyperinflation, political support for renouncing monetary sovereignty, and a recent record of macroeconomic virtue are in the minority and are likely to remain so. The United States should not wish to encourage a premature movement toward dollarization, but at the same time, it can unofficially welcome any countries that find it advantageous.

4 No Single Currency Regime Is Right for All Time

The proposition that the optimal or desirable regime sometimes varies over time may be a harder "sell" than the suggestion that it varies across countries. After all, such criteria as openness and income correlations are called parameters. Does that not imply some permanence? Does not a given economic structure correspond to a given optimal exchange-rate regime for all time?

One answer is that parameters do, in fact, change over time. This point becomes particularly interesting when governments deliberately change their economic structure, for example increasing regional trade integration through regional trading arrangements or even through currency unions. (The endogeneity of the OCA criterion is taken up in Section 5.) Another answer is that recent history seems to suggest that occasional regime switching may be unavoidable for some countries, as messy as such a conclusion must be for central bankers and theorists alike.

Exit Strategies

It is clear that a number of countries that suffered from very high inflation rates, and that underwent repeated unsuccessful stabilization attempts in the 1980s, were eventually able to beat inflation with the aid of exchange-rate targets. Examples are Argentina, Brazil, Mexico, and Israel. In each case, the exchange-rate-based stabilization was highly successful. And yet, in each case, there was enough residual inflation that the currency in subsequent years became progressively overvalued in real terms, putting pressure both on the real economy and on the financial sustainability of the exchange-rate target. How to get out of such a situation gracefully is the challenge of exit strategies.

To say it is a challenge is to say that it is a good topic for research, not that anyone has any convincing answers to suggest as yet.[24] On the one hand, Argentina seems to have done well by sticking with a binding commitment. On the other hand, Israel seems to have done well by introducing more flexibility when its currency became overvalued. Mexico in 1994 and, some will say, Brazil in January 1999 seem to have ended up badly by clinging to their exchange-rate pegs for too long.

For a certain class of high-inflation countries, one is tempted to recommend an initial peg to break the inflationary psychology, followed a few years later by a crawl, or other flexible regime, to cut off overvaluation. But can this advice be right in a model in which people are forward looking? If they know that depreciation is coming in the future, will the stabilization be credible in the present? If it is optimal for the government to incur some real pain to earn inflation-fighting credibility at the beginning, can it really be optimal to give up that credibility after it has been earned?

Perhaps one should factor in political support as a source of variation over time in objectives. Absent public support, the mere proclamation

[24] Eichengreen and Masson (1998) suggest that possible ways to facilitate an orderly exit from a fixed-exchange-rate regime include announcing a substitute nominal anchor for monetary policy, making the transition during a period of tranquility or upward pressure in the currency market, and preannouncing a schedule of band-widening or of increases in the trend of the central parity.

of a fixed-exchange-rate arrangement does not guarantee credibility, notwithstanding the claims of the enthusiasts. This is true even if the commitment is sincerely meant on the part of the president of the central bank; after all, he or she can be fired. Most populations are willing to sacrifice monetary sovereignty in the name of fighting inflation only when hyperinflation is fresh in their minds. In some countries, that may be the length of one or more lifetimes (Germany and Argentina). In others, it might not survive more than a few years into single-digit inflation. Then, an exit strategy might be appropriate.

5 The OCA Criterion Evolves over Time

Such parameters as openness and income correlations are not fixed for all time; they change in response both to the fundamental policy choices countries make and to exogenous factors such as declining transportation costs. Integration is increasing worldwide. Most countries have experienced a large rise in the ratio of trade to income during the postwar period, but this trend is far from having run its course.[25]

The extent of integration among European countries, in particular, is increasing over time, partly as a result of such measures as the removal of barriers to trade and labor mobility in 1992. Even if countries such as the United Kingdom did not satisfy the criteria for joining the optimum currency area in the 1990s, perhaps they will in the future. This point is especially acute for new European Union (EU) members such as Sweden. The long-term effect of EU accession in 1995 will be to promote Sweden's trade with other European countries. Statistical estimates using the gravity model of bilateral trade suggest that membership in the EU increases trade with its members by roughly 60 percent or more (see Frankel, 1997, and Frankel and Wei, 1995, for estimates and other citations to the literature). Thus, Sweden is moving toward the right in Figure 3, making it more likely that it will cross the line and satisfy the OCA criterion in the future than it has in the past.

What about the other parameter, the degree of income correlation among members? We come now to a key point: *Income correlation surely depends on trade integration*. My hypothesis is that this relationship is positive: the more Sweden trades with the EU, the more Swedish

[25] Endogeneity of the degree of wage and price flexibility with respect to the exchange-rate regime has received more attention than endogeneity of trade patterns. The hope that European countries would respond to EMU by moving in the direction of more flexible labor markets, however, "because they will have to," shows no sign so far of being realized. Endogeneity of trade patterns seems more deserving of attention.

FIGURE 3

SWEDEN JOINS THE EU AND EMU

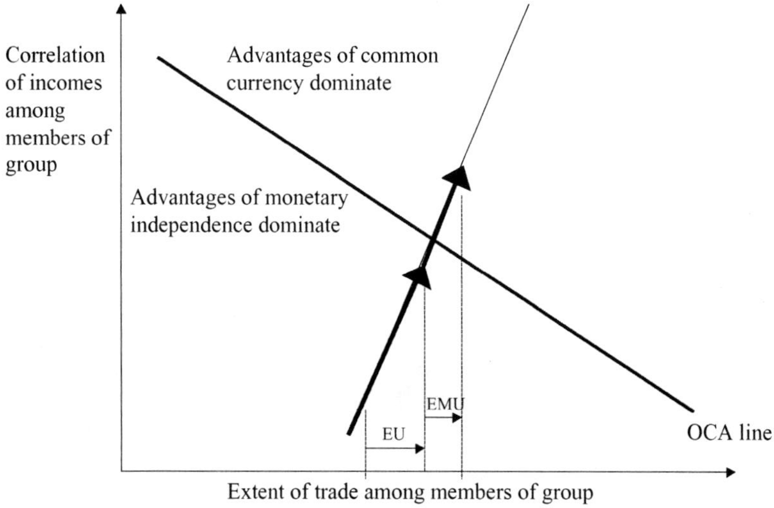

income will be correlated with EU income. (It seems likely that the incomes of U.S. states, for example, are highly correlated with each other because their economies are highly integrated.) The result would be immediate in a demand-driven model, where the correlation of income depends in a simple way on the marginal propensities of the two countries to import from each other, but it could also follow in a variety of other models (for example, productivity shocks spilling over through trade). Thus, I have drawn the correlation function as upward sloping in Figure 3.

Consider what happens when Sweden joins the EU. Not only does trade integration increase, but so does income correlation. It moves up and to the right in Figure 3. The advantages of pegging rise and the disadvantages fall. On both scores, the country comes closer than before to meeting the OCA criterion.

The OCA Criterion Might Be Satisfied Ex Post, Even If Not Ex Ante

Now consider what happens when Sweden decides to join EMU. The elimination of exchange-rate uncertainty and currency-transaction costs further stimulates trade with other EU members. Integration and correlation rise further. The way I have drawn Figure 3, a decision by Sweden to go ahead and join EMU, even though it fails the OCA criterion (given its current structure of trade), would promote trade and raise the income correlation enough to put Sweden over the line. It would satisfy the OCA criterion *ex post*, even though it fails *ex ante*!

The relationship pictured here is not the only one that can come from a consideration of the endogeneity of trade patterns and income correlations. Several authors have pointed out that as trade becomes more highly integrated, countries specialize more in production. These authors then go on to argue that this greater specialization will *reduce* the correlation of incomes.[26] The correlation function would, in that case, slope downward, as it is drawn in Figure 4. An increase in integration would actually move Sweden *away* from the OCA criterion.[27]

FIGURE 4

SWEDEN JOINS THE EU OR EMU, BUT THE EICHENGREEN-KRUGMAN EFFECT DOMINATES

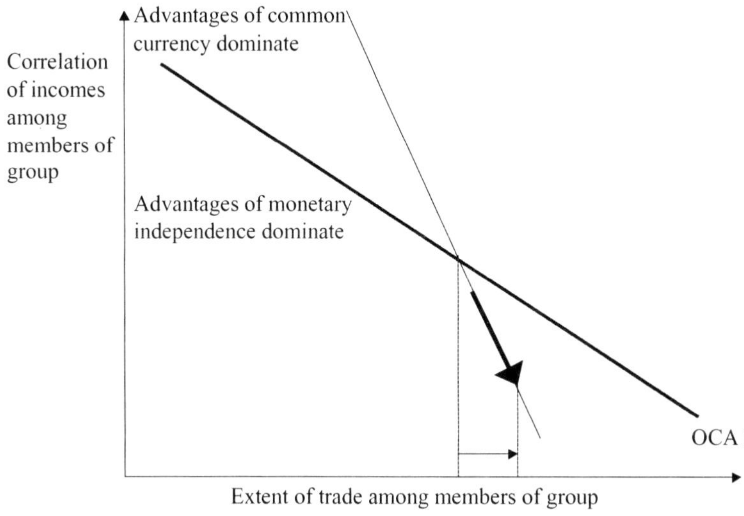

[26] See Eichengreen (1992, pp. 14–16), Krugman (1993, p. 260), and Bayoumi and Eichengreen (1994, pp. 4–5). Their logic may be that only supply shocks matter, and that these will become less correlated as a result of specialization. But if one is going to decompose shocks, as one should in a fully developed theoretical model, one should take into account that monetary independence is more useful for counteracting idiosyncratic demand shocks. There is relatively little that monetary-policy changes can do to counteract supply shocks, though admittedly the same does not apply to other exchange-rate changes.

[27] I have drawn the correlation function as steeper than the OCA line, on the grounds that if economists disagree about whether the slope is positive or negative, the line must be relatively steep. Obviously, this logic is far from tight.

This outcome would hold regardless of whether the increase in integration were a result of exogenous forces such as falling transport costs, a deliberate trade-policy decision such as joining the EU, or a deliberate monetary-policy decision such as joining EMU. At present, I focus on the last. Paul Krugman (1993, p. 260) claims that a country might fail the OCA criterion *ex post*, even if it would pass *ex ante*:

> Theory and the experience of the United States suggest that EC regions will become increasingly specialized, and that as they become more specialized, they will become more vulnerable to region-specific shocks. Regions will, of course, be unable to respond with counter-cyclical monetary or exchange rate policy.

The authors to whom I refer, Barry Eichengreen and Paul Krugman, are not minor figures. Their view that specialization of the economy works against common currencies and that diversification works in favor of it (other things being equal) goes back to Kenen.[28] Although casual empiricism suggests that integration leads to higher correlations, it is certainly possible that the Eichengreen-Krugman view is the right one. There is no substitute for formal empiricism of the sort presented in the next subsection.

For the moment, note an apparent drawback to the Eichengreen-Krugman view that specialization makes countries worse candidates to share a common currency. This drawback derives merely from the logic of drawing boundaries around ever larger geographical areas. Suppose that the joining of two or more regions forms a larger unit that tends to be more highly diversified than the regions are when considered separately. (Recall that trade/GDP falls as size rises.) Then, if an individual region is sufficiently diversified to pass the Eichengreen-Krugman test for pegging its currency to a neighbor, it follows that the larger (more diversified) unit that is thereby created will pass the test by an even wider margin, other things being equal. It will thus want to peg to other neighbors, forming still larger units, and so forth. The process will continue until the entire world is on one currency—quite a corner solution.

What if the individual regions are not sufficiently diversified to begin with to pass the Eichengreen-Krugman criterion? Then, under the OCA logic, they should break up into smaller currency units (say, provinces) that float against each other. But these smaller units will be

[28] Peter Kenen ([1969] 1994) argues that regions that are highly diversified economically are better off (which is clearly true), and that such regions are better candidates to fix their currencies to those of their neighbors than are regions that are more specialized.

even less diversified, will thus fail the Eichengreen-Krugman criterion by a wider margin, and so will decide to break up into still smaller units (say, counties). The process of dissolution will continue until the world is down to the level of the fully specialized individual. In other words, the system is unstable; there exists no interior solution that is an equilibrium. Admittedly, governments might not, in practice, use the OCA criterion in choosing their regime. But it is disturbing to think that if governments do follow the "correct" OCA criterion, the outcome must be either a world of one currency or a world of five billion currencies. This would be an egregious departure from the economist's belief in interior solutions. It doesn't sound right.

The world seems, rather, to consist of intermediate-sized units. They occasionally join together in attempts to form larger currency areas or split apart into smaller ones. The whole, however, is steadily pushed away from the extremes of either overly small, open, specialized currency units, or overly large, closed, diversified units. This finding suggests that regions may be better, rather than worse, candidates for an optimum currency area when they trade a lot with each other.

A Question for Empirical Investigation: Are Trade Links Positively or Negatively Associated with Income Links?

The empirical work reported below is from Frankel and Rose (1998). Its main goal is to ascertain whether income correlation depends positively or negatively on trade integration, that is, whether Figure 3 or Figure 4 best represents the world.

Our basic equation is

$$\text{Corr}(v)_{i,j,t} = a + b\ \text{Trade}(w)_{i,j,t} + e_{i,j,t}\ .$$

$\text{Corr}(v)_{i,j,t}$ is the correlation between country i and country j over time span t for activity concept v. The latter is measured alternatively by various detrended versions of real GDP, industrial production, employment, or the unemployment rate. $\text{Trade}(w)_{i,j,t}$ is the logarithm of the average bilateral trade intensity between country i and country j over time span t using trade intensity concept w. The latter is measured alternatively by bilateral export intensities, bilateral import intensities, or bilateral intensities in total trade—"intensity" refers to the bilateral value divided by the total import or export levels of the two countries.

The error term $e_{i,j,t}$ represents other determinants of bilateral income correlations. The data set includes twenty-one industrial countries annually from 1959 to 1993. The object is to see the sign of the slope coefficient b. It should be negative if the Eichengreen-Krugman specialization effect dominates and positive if our hypothesis is supported. When the activity variable is the change in GDP over four quarters, the coefficient on the intensity of total trade is 0.071. The Huber-White standard error is 0.009. The results are highly significant and tend to bear out our hypothesis that close trade links lead to high income correlations. All sixty combinations of activity and trade measures also give this answer (see Frankel and Rose, 1998). The outcome is the same regardless of the choice of time period, weighting by country size, allowance for nonlinearities, or time-specific or country-specific fixed effects.

A simple ordinary-least-squares (OLS) regression of income correlations on trade intensity may not be appropriate. Countries are likely deliberately to link their currencies to those of some of their most important trading partners. In doing so, they lose the ability to set monetary policy independently of those neighbors, a loss that could, in turn, result in an observed positive association between trade links and income links. The association could thus be the result of the countries' application of the OCA criterion, rather than an aspect of economic structure that is invariant to exchange-rate regime. To identify the effect of bilateral trade patterns on income correlations, we need exogenous determinants of bilateral trade patterns. These can be used as instrumental variables. The preferred set of instrumental variables includes the most basic factors of the well-known gravity model of trade: distance and dummy variables for common borders and common languages.

First-stage linear projections of trade intensity on these three gravity variables show the expected results: significant negative effects of distance and positive effects of common borders or common language. Instrumental variable estimates of our basic equation give estimates of the slope coefficient b that tend to be even higher and more significant statistically than the OLS results. When the activity variable is fourth-differenced on GDP, the coefficient on the intensity of total trade is +0.103. The Huber-White standard error is 0.015. Once again, the results are highly significant and tend to bear out our hypothesis that close trade links lead to high income correlations. As before, the conclusion is robust with respect to choice of activity, trade measures, time period, weighting by country size, allowance for nonlinearities, and time-specific and country-specific fixed effects.

Of the various other extensions we tried, one is particularly important. The Bayoumi-Eichengreen (1994) view is that the high correlation among European countries is a result, not of trade links, but of European countries' decisions to relinquish monetary independence with respect to their neighbors. If this is correct, putting the exchange-rate-regime variable explicitly on the right-hand side of the equation should show that effect, and the apparent effect of the trade and geography variables should disappear. Instead, it turns out that the addition of the exchange-rate variable does not significantly alter *b*.

This outcome bears further theoretical and empirical exploration, but the results appear clearly to show that trade links do, in practice, raise income correlations. It would seem to follow that countries that undergo a gradual rise in trade integration will come gradually over time to satisfy better and better the criteria for a common currency. This effect is just one example of the more general principle that no single exchange-rate regime is right for all time.

6 Summary of Conclusions

Three propositions are currently heard, either as predictions or prescriptions, regarding a country's choice of exchange-rate regime. On the one hand, some veterans of the currency wars yearn for a general move toward increased flexibility. On the other hand, some herald a general move toward reduced flexibility and toward rigid commitments by way of institutional arrangements that lock in fixed rates. These might include currency boards or even the outright disappearance of national currencies in some parts of the world. A third view, which is rapidly becoming a new conventional wisdom, subsumes the first two propositions. It maintains that countries are increasingly finding the middle ground unsustainable and that intermediate regimes such as adjustable pegs, crawling pegs, basket pegs, and target zones are being forced toward the extremes of either a free float or a rigid peg. This hypothesis of the missing middle has yet to be rationalized theoretically. A valid rationale may be that complicated intermediate regimes are insufficiently verifiable or "transparent" to satisfy hard-to-please global investors. It may also be true, however, that no exchange-rate regime would have prevented the recent crises in the emerging-market economies—that the grass may simply look greener at the edges of the pasture than it does in the middle, where the victims had previously been grazing.

One theme of this essay has been that the optimal exchange-rate regime depends on the circumstances of a particular country and time. For some countries, corner solutions are, indeed, good options. Floating will continue to be desirable for large economies. Fixity may be desirable for very small open economies or for those in which a history of hyperinflation or the dominance of finicky global investors has rendered confidence scarce and independent monetary policy no longer usable. For some countries in Latin America, where interest rates currently react more than one for one to the U.S federal funds rate, even full dollarization may be attractive, providing the public is willing politically to give up monetary sovereignty.

But another theme of this essay is that intermediate solutions are more likely to be appropriate for many countries than are corner solutions. This is true, for example, for some developing countries for whom large-scale capital flows are not an issue. For many intermediate emerging-market countries with open capital markets, there is no single regime that is the obvious choice. It is important to remember that in the past, some of these countries have found exchange-rate targets to be a useful component of monetary-stabilization programs when seeking to end a period of high inflation. At other times, however, it has been crucial that the same countries exit from pegs that may have become overvalued, before a crisis develops.

Another dimension for which an intermediate solution is more plausible than a corner solution relates to the geographic area over which it is optimal to have a common currency. The criteria for optimum currency areas include the intensity of trade links and the magnitude of income correlations. Small political units that have tight economic links with their neighbors are too small to float. If the boundaries of a geographic area are drawn large enough that the trade links and income links among its constituent parts are strong compared to the trade links and income links with its neighbors, then it is the optimal size to constitute an independent currency area. Empirical results suggest that when a political unit adopts the currency of a neighbor, the creation of the monetary union promotes trade over time between the neighbors, which in turn has a positive effect on the correlation in incomes. The implication is that the OCA criterion may be satisfied *ex post* even if it fails *ex ante*. This endogeneity of the criterion is another example of the general proposition that the optimal currency regime varies across countries and over time.

References

Alesina, Alberto, and Vittorio Grilli, "The European Central Bank: Reshaping Monetary Politics in Europe," in Matthew B. Canzoneri, Vittorio Grilli, and Paul R. Masson, eds., *Establishing a Central Bank: Issues in Europe and Lessons from the US*, Cambridge and New York, Cambridge University Press, 1992, pp. 49–77.

Bayoumi, Tamim, and Barry Eichengreen, *One Money or Many? Analyzing the Prospects for Monetary Unification in Various Parts of the World*, Princeton Studies in International Finance No. 76, Princeton, N.J., Princeton University, International Finance Section, September 1994.

Calvo, Guillermo, "On Dollarization," Department of Economics, University of Maryland, April 1999, processed.

Corden, W. Max, *Monetary Integration*, Princeton Studies in International Finance, No. 93, Princeton, N.J., Princeton University, International Finance Section, April 1972.

Crockett, Andrew, "Monetary Policy Implications of Increased Capital Flows," in *Changing Capital Markets: Implications for Monetary Policy: A Symposium Sponsored by the Federal Reserve Bank of Kansas City, Jackson Hole, Wyoming, August 19–21, 1994*, Kansas City, Mo., Federal Reserve Bank of Kansas City, 1994, pp. 331–364.

Edison, Hali, and Michael Melvin, "The Determinants and Implications of the Choice of An Exchange Rate System," in William Haraf and Thomas Willett, eds., *Monetary Policy For a Volatile Global Economy*, Washington, D.C., American Enterprise Institute, 1990, pp. 1–44.

Eichengreen, Barry, *Should the Maastricht Treaty Be Saved?* Princeton Studies in International Finance No. 74, Princeton, N.J., Princeton University, International Finance Section, December 1992.

———, *International Monetary Arrangements for the 21st Century*, Washington D.C., Brookings Institution, 1994.

———, "The Only Game in Town," Department of Economics, University of California at Berkeley, November 1998, processed.

Eichengreen, Barry, Paul Masson, and staff, *Exit Strategies: Policy Options for Countries Seeking Greater Exchange Rate Flexibility*, Occasional Paper No. 168, Washington D.C., International Monetary Fund, August 1998.

Engel, Charles, and John Rogers, "How Wide is the Border?" *American Economic Review*, 86 (December 1996), pp. 1112–1125.

———, "Regional Patterns in the Law of One Price: The Role of Geography vs. Currencies," in Jeffrey Frankel, ed., *The Regionalization of the World Economy*, Chicago, University of Chicago Press, 1998, pp. 153–183.

Frankel, Jeffrey, *Regional Trading Blocs*, Washington D.C., Institute for International Economics, 1997.

Frankel, Jeffrey, and Chudozie Okongwu, "Liberalized Portfolio Capital Inflows in Emerging Markets: Sterilization, Expectations, and the Incompleteness of Interest Rate Convergence," *International Journal of Finance and Economics*, 1 (January 1996), pp. 1–23.

Frankel, Jeffrey, and David Romer, "Does Trade Cause Growth?" *American Economic Review*, 89 (June 1999), pp. 379–399.

Frankel, Jeffrey, and Andrew Rose, "The Endogeneity of the Optimum Currency Area Criterion" *Economic Journal*, 108 (July 1998), pp. 1009–1025.

Frankel, Jeffrey, and Shang-Jin Wei, "Emerging Currency Blocs," in Hans Genberg, ed., *The International Monetary System: Its Institutions and Its Future*, Berlin and New York, Springer, 1995, pp. 111–143.

Ghosh, Atish, Anne-Marie Gulde, Jonathan Ostry, and Holger Wolf, "Does the Nominal Exchange Rate Regime Matter?" National Bureau of Economic Research Working Paper No. 5874, Cambridge, Mass., National Bureau of Economic Research, January 1997.

Goldstein, Morris, *The Exchange Rate System and the IMF: A Modest Agenda*, Policy Analyses in International Economics No. 39, Washington, D.C., Institute for International Economics, June 1995.

Hausmann, Ricardo, Michael Gavin, Carmen Pages-Serra, and Ernesto Stein, "Financial Turmoil and the Choice of Exchange Rate Regime," Washington, D.C., Inter-American Development Bank, Research Department, 1999, processed.

Kenen, Peter, "The Theory of Optimum Currency Areas: An Eclectic View," in Kenen, *Exchange Rates and the Monetary System: Selected Essays of Peter B. Kenen*, Aldershot, Elgar, 1994, pp. 3–22 (previously published 1969).

Klein, Michael, and Nancy Marion, "Explaining the Duration of Exchange-Rate Pegs," *Journal of Development Economics*, 54 (December 1997), pp. 387–404.

Krugman, Paul, "Target Zones and Exchange Rate Dynamics," *Quarterly Journal of Economics*, 106 (August 1991), pp. 669–682.

———, "Lessons of Massachusetts for EMU," in Francisco Torres and Francesco Giavazzi, eds., *Adjustment and Growth in the European Monetary Union*, Oxford, New York, and Melbourne, Cambridge University Press, 1993, pp. 241-261.

Larraín, Felipe, and Andrés Velasco, *Exchange-Rate Policy for Emerging Markets: One Size Does Not Fit All*, forthcoming as Essays in International Finance, Princeton. N.J., Princeton University, International Finance Section; draft copy, August 1999.

McCallum, John, "National Borders Matter: Canada-U.S. Regional Trade Patterns," *American Economic Review*, 85 (June 1995), pp. 615–623.

McKinnon, Ronald, "Optimum Currency Areas," *American Economic Review*, 53 (September 1963), pp. 717–724.

Mundell, Robert, "A Theory of Optimum Currency Areas," *American Economic Review*, 51 (September 1961), pp. 657–664.

Obstfeld, Maurice, and Kenneth Rogoff, "The Mirage of Fixed Exchange Rates," *Journal of Economic Perspectives*, 9 (Fall 1995), pp. 73–96.

Romer, David, "Openness and Inflation: Theory and Evidence," *Quarterly Journal of Economics*, 108, (November 1993), pp. 869–903.

Rose, Andrew, "One Money, One Market? The Effect of Common Currencies on International Trade," Haas School of Business, University of California at Berkeley, July 1999, processed.

Summers, Lawrence, Testimony before the Senate Foreign Relations Subcommittee on International Economic Policy and Export/Trade Promotion, U.S. Senate, 106th Congress, 1st Session, January 27, 1999.

Tavlas, George, "The 'New' Theory of Optimal Currency Areas," *World Economy*, 16 (November 1993), pp. 663–685.

Williamson, John, *The Exchange Rate System*, Policy Analyses in International Economics No. 5, Washington, D.C., Institute for International Economics, 2nd ed., June 1985.

———, *What Role for Currency Boards?* Policy Analyses in International Economics No. 40, Washington, D.C., Institute for International Economics, September 1995.

———, *The Crawling Band as an Exchange Rate Regime: Lessons from Chile, Colombia, and Israel*, Washington, D.C., Institute for International Economics, 1996.

FRANK D. GRAHAM MEMORIAL LECTURERS

1950–1951	Milton Friedman
1951–1952	James E. Meade
1952–1953	Sir Dennis Robertson
1953–1954	Paul A. Samuelson
1955–1956	Gottfried Haberler
1956–1957	Ragnar Nurkse
1957–1958	Albert O. Hirschman
1959–1960	Robert Triffin
1960–1961	Jacob Viner
1961–1962	Don Patinkin
1962–1963	Friedrich A. Lutz (Essay 41)
1963–1964	Tibor Scitovsky (Essay 49)
1964–1965	Sir John Hicks
1965–1966	Robert A. Mundell
1966–1967	Jagdish N. Bhagwati (Special Paper 8)
1967–1968	Arnold C. Harberger
1968–1969	Harry G. Johnson
1969–1970	Richard N. Cooper (Essay 86)
1970–1971	W. Max Corden (Essay 93)
1971–1972	Richard E. Caves (Special Paper 10)
1972–1973	Paul A. Volcker
1973–1974	J. Marcus Fleming (Essay 107)
1974–1975	Anne O. Krueger (Study 40)
1975–1976	Ronald W. Jones (Special Paper 12)
1976–1977	Ronald I. McKinnon (Essay 125)
1977–1978	Charles P. Kindleberger (Essay 129)
1978–1979	Bertil Ohlin (Essay 134)
1979–1980	Bela Balassa (Essay 141)
1980–1981	Marina von Neumann Whitman (Essay 143)
1981–1982	Robert E. Baldwin (Essay 150)
1983–1984	Stephen Marris (Essay 155)
1984–1985	Rudiger Dornbusch (Essay 165)
1986–1987	Jacob A. Frenkel (Study 63)
1987–1988	Ronald Findlay (Essay 177)
1988–1989	Michael Bruno (Essay 183)
1988–1989	Elhanan Helpman (Special Paper 16)
1989–1990	Michael L. Mussa (Essay 179)
1990–1991	Toyoo Gyohten
1991–1992	Stanley Fischer
1992–1993	Paul Krugman (Essay 190)
1993–1994	Edward E. Leamer (Study 77)
1994–1995	Jeffrey Sachs
1995–1996	Barry Eichengreen (Essay 198)
1996–1997	Wilfred J. Ethier (Essay 210)
1997–1998	Maurice Obstfeld (Essay 209)
1998–1999	Jeffrey A. Frankel (Essay 215)

PUBLICATIONS OF THE INTERNATIONAL FINANCE SECTION

Notice to Contributors

The International Finance Section publishes papers in four series: ESSAYS IN INTERNATIONAL FINANCE, PRINCETON STUDIES IN INTERNATIONAL FINANCE, and SPECIAL PAPERS IN INTERNATIONAL ECONOMICS contain new work not published elsewhere. REPRINTS IN INTERNATIONAL FINANCE reproduce journal articles previously published by Princeton faculty members associated with the Section. The Section welcomes the submission of manuscripts for publication under the following guidelines:

ESSAYS are meant to disseminate new views about international financial matters and should be accessible to well-informed nonspecialists as well as to professional economists. Technical terms, tables, and charts should be used sparingly; mathematics should be avoided.

STUDIES are devoted to new research on international finance, with preference given to empirical work. They should be comparable in originality and technical proficiency to papers published in leading economic journals. They should be of medium length, longer than a journal article but shorter than a book.

SPECIAL PAPERS are surveys of research on particular topics and should be suitable for use in undergraduate courses. They may be concerned with international trade as well as international finance. They should also be of medium length.

Manuscripts should be submitted in triplicate, typed single sided and double spaced throughout on 8½ by 11 white bond paper. Publication can be expedited if manuscripts are computer keyboarded in WordPerfect or a compatible program. Additional instructions and a style guide are available from the Section.

How to Obtain Publications

The Section's publications are distributed free of charge to college, university, and public libraries and to nongovernmental, nonprofit research institutions. Eligible institutions may ask to be placed on the Section's permanent mailing list.

Individuals and institutions not qualifying for free distribution may receive all publications for the calendar year for a subscription fee of $40.00. Late subscribers will receive all back issues for the year during which they subscribe.

Publications may be ordered individually, with payment made in advance. ESSAYS and REPRINTS cost $9.00 each; STUDIES and SPECIAL PAPERS cost $12.50. An additional $1.50 should be sent for postage and handling within the United States, Canada, and Mexico; $1.75 should be added for surface delivery outside the region.

All payments must be made in U.S. dollars. Subscription fees and charges for single issues will be waived for organizations and individuals in countries where foreign-exchange regulations prohibit dollar payments.

Information about the Section and its publishing program is available at the Section's website at www.princeton.edu/~ifs. A subscription and order form is printed at the end of this volume. Correspondence should be addressed to:

International Finance Section
Department of Economics, Fisher Hall
Princeton University
Princeton, New Jersey 08544-1021
Tel: 609-258-4048 • Fax: 609-258-6419
E-mail: ifs@princeton.edu

List of Recent Publications

A complete list of publications is available at the International Finance Section website at www.princeton.edu/~ifs.

ESSAYS IN INTERNATIONAL FINANCE

177. Ronald Findlay, *The "Triangular Trade" and the Atlantic Economy of the Eighteenth Century: A Simple General-Equilibrium Model.* (March 1990)
178. Alberto Giovannini, *The Transition to European Monetary Union.* (November 1990)
179. Michael L. Mussa, *Exchange Rates in Theory and in Reality.* (December 1990)
180. Warren L. Coats, Jr., Reinhard W. Furstenberg, and Peter Isard, *The SDR System and the Issue of Resource Transfers.* (December 1990)
181. George S. Tavlas, *On the International Use of Currencies: The Case of the Deutsche Mark.* (March 1991)
182. Tommaso Padoa-Schioppa, ed., with Michael Emerson, Kumiharu Shigehara, and Richard Portes, *Europe After 1992: Three Essays.* (May 1991)
183. Michael Bruno, *High Inflation and the Nominal Anchors of an Open Economy.* (June 1991)
184. Jacques J. Polak, *The Changing Nature of IMF Conditionality.* (September 1991)
185. Ethan B. Kapstein, *Supervising International Banks: Origins and Implications of the Basle Accord.* (December 1991)
186. Alessandro Giustiniani, Francesco Papadia, and Daniela Porciani, *Growth and Catch-Up in Central and Eastern Europe: Macroeconomic Effects on Western Countries.* (April 1992)
187. Michele Fratianni, Jürgen von Hagen, and Christopher Waller, *The Maastricht Way to EMU.* (June 1992)
188. Pierre-Richard Agénor, *Parallel Currency Markets in Developing Countries: Theory, Evidence, and Policy Implications.* (November 1992)
189. Beatriz Armendariz de Aghion and John Williamson, *The G-7's Joint-and-Several Blunder.* (April 1993)
190. Paul Krugman, *What Do We Need to Know About the International Monetary System?* (July 1993)
191. Peter M. Garber and Michael G. Spencer, *The Dissolution of the Austro-Hungarian Empire: Lessons for Currency Reform.* (February 1994)
192. Raymond F. Mikesell, *The Bretton Woods Debates: A Memoir.* (March 1994)
193. Graham Bird, *Economic Assistance to Low-Income Countries: Should the Link be Resurrected?* (July 1994)
194. Lorenzo Bini-Smaghi, Tommaso Padoa-Schioppa, and Francesco Papadia, *The Transition to EMU in the Maastricht Treaty.* (November 1994)
195. Ariel Buira, *Reflections on the International Monetary System.* (January 1995)
196. Shinji Takagi, *From Recipient to Donor: Japan's Official Aid Flows, 1945 to 1990 and Beyond.* (March 1995)
197. Patrick Conway, *Currency Proliferation: The Monetary Legacy of the Soviet Union.* (June 1995)
198. Barry Eichengreen, *A More Perfect Union? The Logic of Economic Integration.* (June 1996)

199. Peter B. Kenen, ed., with John Arrowsmith, Paul De Grauwe, Charles A. E. Goodhart, Daniel Gros, Luigi Spaventa, and Niels Thygesen, *Making EMU Happen—Problems and Proposals: A Symposium.* (August 1996)
200. Peter B. Kenen, ed., with Lawrence H. Summers, William R. Cline, Barry Eichengreen, Richard Portes, Arminio Fraga, and Morris Goldstein, *From Halifax to Lyons: What Has Been Done about Crisis Management?* (October 1996)
201. Louis W. Pauly, *The League of Nations and the Foreshadowing of the International Monetary Fund.* (December 1996)
202. Harold James, *Monetary and Fiscal Unification in Nineteenth-Century Germany: What Can Kohl Learn from Bismarck?* (March 1997)
203. Andrew Crockett, *The Theory and Practice of Financial Stability.* (April 1997)
204. Benjamin J. Cohen, *The Financial Support Fund of the OECD: A Failed Initiative.* (June 1997)
205. Robert N. McCauley, *The Euro and the Dollar.* (November 1997)
206. Thomas Laubach and Adam S. Posen, *Disciplined Discretion: Monetary Targeting in Germany and Switzerland.* (December 1997)
207. Stanley Fischer, Richard N. Cooper, Rudiger Dornbusch, Peter M. Garber, Carlos Massad, Jacques J. Polak, Dani Rodrik, and Savak S. Tarapore, *Should the IMF Pursue Capital-Account Convertibility?* (May 1998)
208. Charles P. Kindleberger, *Economic and Financial Crises and Transformations in Sixteenth-Century Europe.* (June 1998)
209. Maurice Obstfeld, *EMU: Ready or Not?* (July 1998)
210. Wilfred Ethier, *The International Commercial System.* (September 1998)
211. John Williamson and Molly Mahar, *A Survey of Financial Liberalization.* (November 1998)
212. Ariel Buira, *An Alternative Approach to Financial Crises.* (February 1999)
213. Barry Eichengreen, Paul Masson, Miguel Savastano, and Sunil Sharma, *Transition Strategies and Nominal Anchors on the Road to Greater Exchange-Rate Flexibility.* (April 1999)
214. Curzio Giannini, *"Enemy of None but a Common Friend of All"? An International Perspective on the Lender-of-Last-Resort Function.* (June 1999)
215. Jeffrey A. Frankel, *No Single Currency Regime Is Right for All Countries or at All Times.* (August 1999)

PRINCETON STUDIES IN INTERNATIONAL FINANCE

66. Helmut Reisen, *Public Debt, External Competitiveness, and Fiscal Discipline in Developing Countries.* (November 1989)
67. Victor Argy, Warwick McKibbin, and Eric Siegloff, *Exchange-Rate Regimes for a Small Economy in a Multi-Country World.* (December 1989)
68. Mark Gersovitz and Christina H. Paxson, *The Economies of Africa and the Prices of Their Exports.* (October 1990)
69. Felipe Larraín and Andrés Velasco, *Can Swaps Solve the Debt Crisis? Lessons from the Chilean Experience.* (November 1990)
70. Kaushik Basu, *The International Debt Problem, Credit Rationing and Loan Pushing: Theory and Experience.* (October 1991)

71. Daniel Gros and Alfred Steinherr, *Economic Reform in the Soviet Union: Pas de Deux between Disintegration and Macroeconomic Destabilization*. (November 1991)
72. George M. von Furstenberg and Joseph P. Daniels, *Economic Summit Declarations, 1975-1989: Examining the Written Record of International Cooperation*. (February 1992)
73. Ishac Diwan and Dani Rodrik, *External Debt, Adjustment, and Burden Sharing: A Unified Framework*. (November 1992)
74. Barry Eichengreen, *Should the Maastricht Treaty Be Saved?* (December 1992)
75. Adam Klug, *The German Buybacks, 1932-1939: A Cure for Overhang?* (November 1993)
76. Tamim Bayoumi and Barry Eichengreen, *One Money or Many? Analyzing the Prospects for Monetary Unification in Various Parts of the World*. (September 1994)
77. Edward E. Leamer, *The Heckscher-Ohlin Model in Theory and Practice*. (February 1995)
78. Thorvaldur Gylfason, *The Macroeconomics of European Agriculture*. (May 1995)
79. Angus S. Deaton and Ronald I. Miller, *International Commodity Prices, Macroeconomic Performance, and Politics in Sub-Saharan Africa*. (December 1995)
80. Chander Kant, *Foreign Direct Investment and Capital Flight*. (April 1996)
81. Gian Maria Milesi-Ferretti and Assaf Razin, *Current-Account Sustainability*. (October 1996)
82. Pierre-Richard Agénor, *Capital-Market Imperfections and the Macroeconomic Dynamics of Small Indebted Economies*. (June 1997)
83. Michael Bowe and James W. Dean, *Has the Market Solved the Sovereign-Debt Crisis?* (August 1997)
84. Willem H. Buiter, Giancarlo M. Corsetti, and Paolo A. Pesenti, *Interpreting the ERM Crisis: Country-Specific and Systemic Issues*. (March 1998)
85. Holger C. Wolf, *Transition Strategies: Choices and Outcomes*. (June 1999)
86. Alessandro Prati and Garry J. Schinasi, *Financial Stability in European Economic and Monetary Union*. (August 1999)

SPECIAL PAPERS IN INTERNATIONAL ECONOMICS

16. Elhanan Helpman, *Monopolistic Competition in Trade Theory*. (June 1990)
17. Richard Pomfret, *International Trade Policy with Imperfect Competition*. (August 1992)
18. Hali J. Edison, *The Effectiveness of Central-Bank Intervention: A Survey of the Literature After 1982*. (July 1993)
19. Sylvester W.C. Eijffinger and Jakob De Haan, *The Political Economy of Central-Bank Independence*. (May 1996)

REPRINTS IN INTERNATIONAL FINANCE

28. Peter B. Kenen, *Ways to Reform Exchange-Rate Arrangements*; reprinted from *Bretton Woods: Looking to the Future*, 1994. (November 1994)
29. Peter B. Kenen, *Sorting Out Some EMU Issues*; reprinted from Jean Monnet Chair Paper 38, Robert Schuman Centre, European University Institute, 1996. (December 1996)

fold over, seal, and send

◦ SUBSCRIBE ◦ ORDER ◦

INTERNATIONAL FINANCE SECTION

Subscriptions

Rate $40 a year

The International Finance Section issues six to eight publications each year in a mix of Essays, Studies, and occasional Special Papers and Reprints. Late subscribers receive all publications for the subscription year. Prepayment is required and may be made by check in U.S. dollars or by Visa or MasterCard. A complete list of publications is available at www.princeton.edu/~ifs.

Address inquiries to:

International Finance Section
Department of Economics, Fisher Hall
Princeton University
Princeton, NJ 08544–1021

Book Orders

Essays & Reprints	$9.00
Studies & Special Papers	$12.50

plus postage

Within U.S.	$1.50
Outside U.S. (surface mail)	$1.75

Discounts are available for book dealers and for orders of five or more publications.

Telephone: 609–258–4048
Telefax: 609–258–6419
E-mail: ifs@princeton.edu

fold up

INTERNATIONAL FINANCE SECTION

This is a subscription ☐ ; a book order ☐

Essay #(s) _____, _____ No. of copies___

Study #(s) _____, _____ No. of copies___

Special Paper # _____ No. of copies___

Reprint # _____ No. of copies___

☐ Enclosed is my check made payable to Princeton University, International Finance Section

totaling $_____________.

Please charge: ☐ Visa ☐ MasterCard

Acct.# ______________________________

Expires ______________________________

Signature______________________________

Send to:

Name______________________________

Address______________________________

City______________________________

State ________________Zip __________

Country______________________________

FIRST
CLASS
POSTAGE
HERE

INTERNATIONAL FINANCE SECTION
DEPARTMENT OF ECONOMICS
FISHER HALL
PRINCETON UNIVERSITY
PRINCETON, NJ 08544-1021